SUMMER'S BLOODIEST DAYS

THE BATTLE OF GETTYSBURG AS TOLD FROM ALL SIDES

BY JENNIFER L. WEBER
FOREWORD BY JAMES M. MCPHERSON

 NATIONAL GEOGRAPHIC

WASHINGTON, D.C.

Visit us online at www.nationalgeographic.com/books

For librarians and teachers: www.ngchildrensbooks.org

More for kids from National Geographic: kids.nationalgeographic.com

For information about special discounts for bulk purchases, please contact National Geographic Books Special Sales: ngspecsales@ngs.org

For rights or permissions inquiries, please contact National Geographic Books Subsidiary Rights: ngbookrights@ngs.org

Library of Congress Cataloging-in-Publication Data
Weber, Jennifer L., 1962–
Summer's bloodiest days : the Battle of Gettysburg as told from all sides / by Jennifer L. Weber; foreword by James M. McPherson. — 1st ed.
p. cm.
Includes bibliographical references and index.
ISBN 978-1-4263-0706-5 (hardcover : alk. paper)
ISBN 978-1-4263-0707-2 (library binding : alk. paper)
1. Gettysburg, Battle of, Gettysburg, Pa., 1863—Juvenile literature. I. Title.
  E475.53.W43 2010
  973.7'349—dc22
            2009048213
Scholastic edition
ISBN: 978-1-4263-0808-6
Printed in China
10/RRDS/1

Published by the National Geographic Society
John M. Fahey, Jr., *President and Chief Executive Officer*
Gilbert M. Grosvenor, *Chairman of the Board*
Tim T. Kelly, *President, Global Media Group*
John Q. Griffin, *President, Publishing*
Nina D. Hoffman, *Executive Vice President, President of Book Publishing Group*
Melina Gerosa Bellows, *Executive Vice President of Children's Publishing*

Prepared by the Book Division
Nancy Laties Feresten, *Vice President, Editor in Chief, Children's Books*
Jonathan Halling, *Design Director, Children's Publishing*
Jennifer Emmett, *Executive Editor, Reference and Solo, Children's Books*
Carl Mehler, *Director of Maps*
R. Gary Colbert, *Production Director*
Jennifer A. Thornton, *Managing Editor*

Staff for This Book
Suzanne Patrick Fonda, *Project Editor*
Eva Absher, *Art Direction and Design*
Lori Epstein, *Illustrations Editor*
Priyanka Lamichhane, *Associate Editor*
Kate Olesin, *Editorial Assistant*
Martin S. Walz, *Map Research and Production*
Grace Hill, *Associate Managing Editor*
Lewis R. Bassford, *Production Manager*
Susan Borke, *Legal and Business Affairs*

Manufacturing and Quality Management
Christopher A. Liedel, *Chief Financial Officer*
Phillip L. Schlosser, *Vice President*
Chris Brown, *Technical Director*
Nicole Elliott, *Manufacturing Manager*
Rachel Faulise, *Manufacturing Manager*

ACKNOWLEDGMENTS

— In memory of Aunt Alma, Aunt Delma, and Cap —

A book is a collaborative effort, and I am grateful for all those who helped me with this one. Besides the staff of National Geographic Children's Books (especially Suzanne Fonda, Eva Absher, Lori Epstein, and Martin Walz), I relied on several people more familiar than I with kids' literature to let me know if I was on the right track. Librarian Marge Huskins gave me tremendous early input, but the kids who read the manuscript were the most telling audience. Many thanks to Albert and Sarah Muzquiz, Michael and David Willigrod, and Jack Buyske for their time, their smart comments, and their good insights. Thanks also to Jeremy Prichard for his sharp work checking quotations and sources.

James M. McPherson, my mentor and friend, backed me up on this project by helping me make sense of a swirling, chaotic battle, reviewing the text, and writing the Foreword. I also appreciate the comments of Scott Hartwig, Supervisory Historian, Gettysburg National Military Park. Any errors that may have crept into the book remain entirely my own.

Many friends and family members provided much moral support. I lost five of them as I worked on this project. My aunt, Marie Balske, was a lively and generous woman committed to family; Richard Kassebaum was a talented filmmaker with whom I loved talking politics; Bill Lagan was simply one of the nicest people anyone could ever hope to meet; Joanne Cominsky Scoville, a loyal friend since childhood, was always willing to listen and lend a helping hand; and finally my mom, who always, *always* stood behind me. Aunt Alma, Aunt Delma, and Captain Gooderidge, to whom this book is dedicated, died long ago, but they were closer to me than my own grandparents, whose role they filled. I miss you all terribly.

Cover: *Colonel Joshua Chamberlain of the 20th Maine Regiment leads his men in a charge down Little Round Top. His actions helped save the far left of the Union line on the second day of battle.*

Case Cover: *Lincoln's Gettysburg Address overlays Mort Künstler's painting of General Lewis Armistead leading his Virginians toward the Yankee line on Cemetery Ridge July 3.*

Endsheets: *Confederate (front) and Union flags overlay a map of Gettysburg battlefield compiled by W.F. Goodhue, published in 1863.*

Title Page: *Hand-to-hand fighting was rare during the Civil War, but it took place briefly several times at Gettysburg, including at the Angle on Cemetery Ridge during Pickett's Charge (shown here).*

TABLE OF CONTENTS

FOREWORD 8

PROLOGUE
THE MEANING OF GETTYSBURG 10

CHAPTER 1
THE ROAD TO GETTYSBURG 14

CHAPTER 2
THE BATTLE: DAY ONE 21

CHAPTER 3
THE BATTLE: DAY TWO 31

CHAPTER 4
THE BATTLE: DAY THREE 40

CHAPTER 5
AFTERMATH 53

TIME LINE 58

RESOURCES 59

QUOTE SOURCES 60

ILLUSTRATION CREDITS 60

INDEX 61

Following orders from Captain Hubert Dilger, Ohio artillerymen race to move two cannon into firing position against Confederate guns on Oak Hill on the afternoon of July 1.

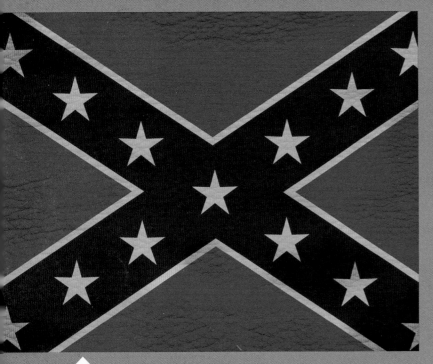

The Confederate battle flag had 13 stars, representing the 11 states of the Confederacy plus Kentucky and Missouri, two Border States with strong Southern sympathies.

Thousands of young people tour the Gettysburg battlefield every year. They come on field trips with high school or middle school classmates. They visit with their parents on summer vacations. More than 2,000 college students have walked the hallowed ground of Gettysburg with me over the past 30 years.

What brings so many people to this battlefield in rural Pennsylvania? Why do they look with wonder and awe on such places made famous in those first three days of July 1863: the Peach Orchard, Devil's Den, the Wheatfield, Little Round Top, Seminary Ridge, Cemetery Hill, Culp's Hill, and Cemetery Ridge? Part of the answer lies in the terrible but heroic drama of those three days in which 11,000 soldiers were killed and another 30,000 wounded—the bloodiest battle of the Civil War and, indeed, in the history of the Western Hemisphere. I have seen many visitors shed tears or stand in silent tribute to the courage and sacrifice of the 165,000 Union and Confederate soldiers who fought there. No other historical site evokes such emotion and reverence.

Yet the meaning of Gettysburg transcends the momentous story of the fighting. Great events hinged on the outcome of the battle. A victory by General Robert E. Lee's Army of Northern Virginia might have led to Confederate independence. The United States might have remained broken into two nations, with incalculable consequences for the history of America—and the world. But General Lee's effort to conquer a peace on Northern soil failed. General George G. Meade's Army of the Potomac forced Lee's crippled army back to Virginia. The victory, coupled with the capture of the Confederate bastion of Vicksburg on the Mississippi River one day after the Battle of Gettysburg ended, gave the Union cause an enormous boost.

Although the war went on for almost two more years, Gettysburg was a crucial turning point toward ultimate Union victory. And that victory meant more than preservation of the United States as one nation. It also meant the abolition of slavery—the institution that had divided the country since its founding. President Abraham Lincoln said it best in his brief address on November 19, 1863, to dedicate the cemetery for Union soldiers killed at Gettysburg. The battle not only helped ensure that the United States would not "perish from the earth," but also gave the nation "a new birth of freedom."

In the pages that follow, Jennifer Weber narrates the thrilling story of Gettysburg in words and pictures. Whether you have already been to Gettysburg, intend to go, or just enjoy a good book, you will find the reading of this one to be a richly rewarding experience.

James M. McPherson

This U.S. flag includes a star for West Virginia, which separated from Virginia and was admitted as the 35th state on June 20, 1863.

THE MEANING OF GETTYSBURG

> " **FOURSCORE AND SEVEN YEARS AGO,...** "
>
> —ABRAHAM LINCOLN, GETTYSBURG ADDRESS

Abraham
Lincoln

...our fathers brought forth on this continent, a new nation, conceived in Liberty, and dedicated to the proposition that all men are created equal.

Now we are engaged in a great civil war, testing whether that nation, or any nation so conceived and so dedicated, can long endure. We are met on a great battlefield of that war. We have come to dedicate a portion of that field, as a final resting place for those who here gave their lives that that nation might live. It is altogether fitting and proper that we should do this.

But in a larger sense, we can not dedicate—we can not consecrate—we can not hallow—this ground. The brave men, living and dead, who struggled here, have consecrated it, far above our poor power to add or detract. The world will little note, nor long remember *what we say here, but it can never forget what they did here. It is for us the living, rather, to be dedicated here to the unfinished work which they who fought here have thus far so nobly advanced. It is rather for us to be here dedicated to the great task remaining before us—that from these honored dead we take increased devotion to that cause for which they here gave the last full measure of devotion—that we here highly resolve that these dead shall not have died in vain— that this nation, under God, shall have a new birth of freedom—and that government of the people, by the people, for the people, shall not perish from the earth.*

Local attorney David Wills was appointed to create a cemetery for slain Union soldiers. About a month before the dedication ceremony he sent out this request for bids to bury the dead.

On November 19, 1863, President Abraham Lincoln delivered his Gettysburg Address in honor of the Union (Northern) soldiers who had died four and a half months earlier in the biggest battle ever to take place on the continent. Lincoln was not the main speaker at the dedication of the national cemetery in Gettysburg, Pennsylvania. In fact, David Wills, the local attorney responsible for organizing the event, had not invited the President until November 2 and had asked him only to make

PROPOSALS
FOR THE REMOVAL OF THE DEAD ON THE
GETTYSBURG BATTLE-FIELD.

SEALED proposals will be received at my Office in the Borough of Gettysburg, until the 22d inst., at 12 o'clock, noon, for the following two contracts, viz:

1st. For disinterring the bodies on the Gettysburg Battle Field and at the Hospitals in the vicinity, and removing them to the Soldiers' Cemetery on the south side of the Borough of Gettysburg.
2d. For digging the graves, and burying the dead in the Cemetery.

☞The specifications of work for each contract, to be strictly complied with by the Contractor, can be seen and examined at my office.

DAVID WILLS,

Gettysburg, Oct. 15, 1863.   Agent for A. G. CURTIN, Governor of Pennsylvania.

PRINTED AT THE "SENTINEL OFFICE," GETTYSBURG.

THE UNION AND THE CONFEDERACY

CANADA

WASH. TERR.

OREGON

NEV. TERR.

CALIF.

DAKOTA TERRITORY

MINN.

WIS.

MICH.

NEBRASKA TERRITORY

IOWA

UTAH TERR.

COLORADO TERRITORY

KANS.

NEW MEXICO TERRITORY

INDIAN TERR.

MO.

ILL.

IND.

OHIO

PA.

N.Y.

VT.

N.H.

ME.

MASS.

R.I.

CONN.

N.J.

DEL.

MD.

W. VA.

VA.

KY.

TENN.

N.C.

ARK.

MISS.

ALA.

GA.

S.C.

Boundary of Confederacy

TEXAS

LA.

FLA.

MEXICO

- Union free state
- Union slave state (Border States)
- Slave state seceding before Fort Sumter, April 1861
- Slave state seceding after Fort Sumter, April 1861
- Territory

0   400 mi
0   600 km

This map shows the boundary (red line) between the Union and the Confederacy. Border States (light blue) were slave states that stayed in the Union.

"a few appropriate remarks." Lincoln had a grander purpose.

By the time of the Gettysburg Address, the Civil War had been going on for two and a half years. Lincoln's Emancipation Proclamation, which freed slaves in areas not under Union control, had gone into effect ten months earlier, on January 1, 1863. He wanted to remind Northerners

what they were fighting for, what the stakes were in this war. The Declaration of Independence, which Thomas Jefferson had written 87 years earlier (the "fourscore and seven years ago" Lincoln alludes to), had asserted that "all men are created equal." It did not specify only white men, but as long as slavery existed, the nation could not fulfill its promise of equality. Nor could the country deliver on another promise made in the Declaration: freedom.

The Civil War was not just about freeing the slaves or equality for all, though. It was also a war to preserve the nation. The United States at the time was one of only two countries on Earth with a government elected by the people. The other was Switzerland. Monarchs or tyrants ran other nations. If the North lost the Civil War,

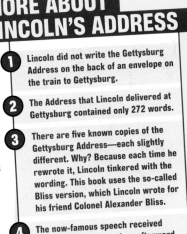

MORE ABOUT LINCOLN'S ADDRESS

1. Lincoln did not write the Gettysburg Address on the back of an envelope on the train to Gettysburg.

2. The Address that Lincoln delivered at Gettysburg contained only 272 words.

3. There are five known copies of the Gettysburg Address—each slightly different. Why? Because each time he rewrote it, Lincoln tinkered with the wording. This book uses the so-called Bliss version, which Lincoln wrote for his friend Colonel Alexander Bliss.

4. The now-famous speech received mixed reviews in the days afterward.

5. The speech was so short that a photographer on the scene did not have enough time to record the moment.

CIVIL WAR PHOTOGRAPHS

Photography had been around since the 1830s but didn't begin to realize its full potential until the Civil War. Thousands of soldiers had their pictures taken in uniform for the folks at home. Mathew Brady, the most famous photographer of the age, created a sensation in 1862 when he exhibited photos of dead bodies on the battlefield at Antietam. It was the first time Americans had seen the consequences of war in such stark and violent terms. Photos of actual battles were not possible because any movement during the long exposure time created a blurred image. Some photos were staged, as when corpses were moved to heighten the emotional impact on the viewer.

Lincoln and many others thought the experiment in government that George Washington and John Adams and Thomas Jefferson had launched would fail. The Yankees had to press on, had to win if the nation were to survive. The best way to honor the thousands of men who fell at Gettysburg, Lincoln said, was to continue fighting.

This photograph of the dedication ceremony at Gettysburg was considered just another blurry crowd scene until a researcher recognized Lincoln. He and others on the stage are less blurred because they were seated or standing still.

When the war was won, the country would be reborn as one that lived up to Jefferson's promises of equality and freedom, and the American experiment in government would go on.

The message that Lincoln delivered in less than three minutes has become one of the cornerstones of American democracy. Often quoted, it is now as familiar as the Declaration of Independence or the preamble to the Constitution. To appreciate Lincoln's words fully, we must understand the bloodshed, the fear, the heroism, and the suffering that took place at Gettysburg in July 1863.

THE ROAD TO GETTYSBURG

"MY FEET HURT ME VERY MUCH"

—CORPORAL SAMUEL PICKENS,
5TH ALABAMA REGIMENT

The Union blockade of Southern ports led to all kinds of shortages in the Confederacy, including shoes.

Robert E. Lee's Army of Northern Virginia—one of several armies serving the Confederacy—was on the march in June 1863. The hardships for the men of Company D, 5th Alabama Regiment were about what they always were. They were walking about 20 miles a day. They slept in the rain, sometimes out in the open and sometimes under a leaky tent roof. It didn't seem to matter where they were; army life was primitive and uncomfortable. "Before the war I would have thought it would kill a man to lie all night in wet clothes, but soldiers can stand anything," wrote Corporal Samuel Pickens. Pickens, who was from near Greensboro, Alabama, had known little discomfort before the war. He was heir to one of Alabama's greatest cotton fortunes, had attended the University of Virginia, and his family owned more than 200 slaves. Now his feet were so wet he could not get his shoes and socks on, so he went without socks. He had sore feet and asked the regimental surgeon if he could hop a ride on an ambulance rather than walk. But so many men had sore feet that the doctor turned him down. The ambulances were saved for men suffering from fever.

A victory at Chancellorsville against a
Union army twice the size of his own gave
Robert E. Lee the confidence to move into
the North. Here, a regimental band heralds
the passing of Lee and his staff.

UNION INFANTRYMAN

- Forage cap, or kepi (a French word meaning "cap")
- Blanket roll
- Frying pan
- American-made musket
- Strap for haversack, which carried food and was worn on the left hip
- Machine or hand sewn woolen fatigue blouse with brass buttons worn with wool pants
- Leather cartridge box and percussion cap box
- Knapsack for personal items, tent, extra clothing, and extra ammunition. The sack could weigh as much as 40 pounds.
- Leather shoes

Despite the hardships, Lee's army was in high spirits. In early May it had scored a spectacular victory at Chancellorsville, Virginia—a battle in which the 5th Alabama had played a critical role. The Army of the Potomac, one of several Northern armies, had outnumbered the Rebel forces nearly two to one, but Confederates had thrashed the Yankees anyway. The defeat was just the latest humiliation for the Army of the Potomac. **CHANCELLORSVILLE WAS A DEFINING MOMENT FOR LEE. HE CAME AWAY FROM THAT BATTLE BELIEVING THAT HIS ARMY WAS INVINCIBLE.** He also thought that if he could follow up on Chancellorsville with another big and decisive win, Northerners might withdraw their support for the war, give Confederates their independence, and the war would be over. With that in mind, he started marching north in early June.

The travel was hard on Lee's men. They had been surviving on reduced rations for some time and their wool uniforms caused many of them to faint or suffer heatstroke. By the end of June the army had marched from Virginia into Maryland and from Maryland into southern

Pennsylvania. "I was completely broken down & my feet hurt me very much," Pickens wrote. He did not mention the condition of his shoes, but many of the Rebels were barefoot or their shoes were falling apart. The good news was that they were in the North, where the land was nearly untouched by war and where food was plentiful: cherries, chickens, cattle, and "some Dutch bread—'preatzel' or some such name—rolled out round—the size of your finger & smaller—glazed over & pretty salt," Pickens wrote.

Spread across an arc 45 miles long, Lee's army caused widespread panic in lower Pennsylvania. Residents knew that the state militia could not defeat such a large force without the help of the Army of the Potomac, which was to the south in Maryland. In an effort to protect their animals from marauding Rebels, many farmers gathered their livestock and left the area. While white Pennsylvanians had reason to be concerned about their property, black Pennsylvanians had cause to be terrified for their lives. They knew that Southern troops often rounded up African Americans— regardless of whether they were legally free (blacks who either had not been born slaves, had bought their way out of

CONFEDERATE INFANTRYMAN

Forage cap, or kepi, although many preferred a broader brimmed slouch hat as protection against the sun and rain

Socket bayonet

Cloth-and-leather knapsack imported from England

Wooden canteen with iron straps

Gray jacket and trousers locally made from a wool-cotton mix; shortages caused this to be replaced by the so-called butter-nut uniform, made of homespun cloth colored with dye from crushed butternuts.

Leather cartridge box

Leather percussion cap box

Tin coffee cup

Haversack for carrying food

English rifle

Leather shoes

slavery, or had been freed by their masters) or runaway slaves—and sent them south into bondage. News of approaching Confederates sent most African Americans fleeing like deer before a fire.

By the time a scouting party of Confederates under the command of General Jubal Early arrived in Gettysburg on June 26, many of the town's 2,400 residents had left. This prosperous commercial center and its surrounding farms were now occupied mainly by women, children, and the elderly. The look of the weary Rebel soldiers shocked Fannie Buehler, wife of one of the town's newspaper editors. She said she had never seen "a more unsightly set of men, and as I looked at them in their dirty, torn garments, hatless, shoeless, and foot-sore, I pitied them from the depth of my heart."

The Rebels were looking for money and supplies. They did their business quickly

CONFEDERATE MONEY

Lee tried to keep Northern farmers and merchants from being too upset with his men by ordering his troops to pay for any food and supplies they took. The problem was that Lee's soldiers carried only Confederate money. The currency had no value in the North and less and less in the South, where the solution to raising more money was simply to print more. As a result, goods that once cost $2 soared to $20 or more. Even so, Southerners went to great lengths to preserve their increasingly worthless notes. The $5 bill below is glued together with a 10-cent note, while rips in a $10 bill are doctored with a pin and a stamp.

and got out of town, but their brief stay may have changed the course of history. Some historians believe Lee's army, in need of replenishing its stockpile of shoes for the infantry after the long march north, may have learned about the town's several tanneries and 22 shoemakers from Early's expedition. In truth, those 22 cobblers could barely keep the residents of Adams County shod. Nevertheless, **IT IS POSSIBLE THAT THE ARMY OF NORTHERN VIRGINIA CAME TO GETTYSBURG IN SEARCH OF SHOES, NOT A FIGHT.**

One thing historians do know is that Lee was operating without any input from his cavalry during most of the march that took him into Pennsylvania. Cavalrymen, who could move quickly on their horses, served as

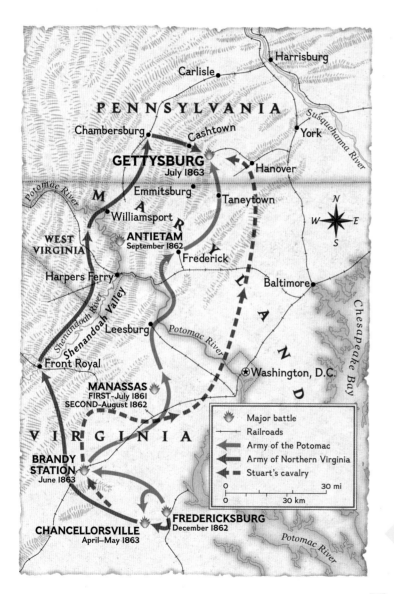

"Jeb" Stuart

the army's "eyes" by scouting out the enemy and the terrain (the hills, valleys, woods, fields, streams—any geographic feature that could work to the army's advantage or disadvantage). Lee had a superb cavalry, led by General James Ewell Brown ("Jeb") Stuart. Stuart had been embarrassed by the Yankees' surprise attack at Brandy Station, Virginia, on June 9 as the Confederates made their way north after Chancellorsville. In an effort to redeem himself, Stuart set out to circle the Army of the Potomac. He did this with Lee's blessing so long as he stayed in communication with the main army. But Stuart failed to do this. Without Stuart, Lee was operating blind. On June 30, as Lee joined the bulk of his army at Cashtown, eight miles west of Gettysburg, he had no idea that he was about to run smack into the Army of the Potomac.

Mountains edging the Shenandoah Valley helped shield Lee's movements as he headed north. This, the need to protect Washington, D.C., and Stuart's cavalry hampered the Union army's pursuit.

Standing on McPherson Ridge, Union cavalry commander John Buford points out Confederates across Willoughby Run to General John Reynolds (on horseback with binoculars).

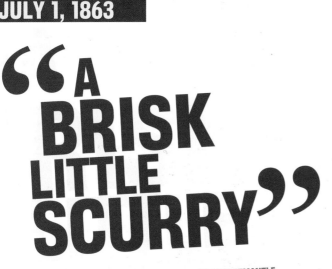

"A BRISK LITTLE SCURRY"

—ARTHUR FREEMANTLE,
BRITISH OBSERVER

Officers and scouts relied on field glasses to see the enemy or follow action on the battlefield from a distance.

The sun rising over Gettysburg on July 1, 1863, turned the eastern sky red. The fields outside of town were orderly, the houses tidy, and the wood-and-stone barns large and well built. The land folded itself into a series of ridges—Cemetery, Seminary, McPherson—that stretched from Gettysburg west to the South Mountains. Just southeast of town stood Culp's Hill, and due south, almost three miles away, were the two most prominent geographic features in the area: Little Round Top and Big Round Top. Nothing at dawn indicated that by day's end the largest battle ever fought on the North American continent would be in full force.

Confederate General Henry Heth (pronounced Heath), responding to a report that Yankee militia had been spotted to the east, was leading two brigades from Cashtown down the Chambersburg Pike. Heth said after the war that he was looking for shoes when he headed to Gettysburg on July 1, but his main mission was to secure the town's rail line and ten major roads before Union soldiers could gain a foothold there.

Ahead of them atop McPherson Ridge were 2,700 Union cavalry soldiers under the command of General John Buford.

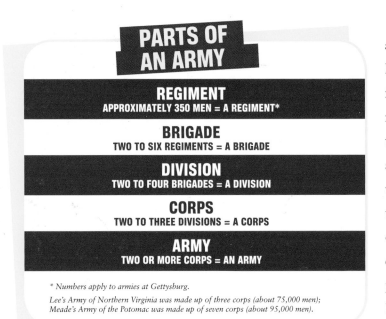

PARTS OF AN ARMY

REGIMENT
APPROXIMATELY 350 MEN = A REGIMENT*

BRIGADE
TWO TO SIX REGIMENTS = A BRIGADE

DIVISION
TWO TO FOUR BRIGADES = A DIVISION

CORPS
TWO TO THREE DIVISIONS = A CORPS

ARMY
TWO OR MORE CORPS = AN ARMY

* Numbers apply to armies at Gettysburg.
Lee's Army of Northern Virginia was made up of three corps (about 75,000 men);
Meade's Army of the Potomac was made up of seven corps (about 95,000 men).

George G. Meade

about 7:30 a.m., and skirmishing followed. Looking for a better view of the fight, Buford raced to the top of the nearby Lutheran Theological Seminary, the highest point around. The situation appeared dire. Buford dashed off a note to General George G. Meade to report that "the enemy's force are advancing on me at this point and driving my picketts and skirmishers very rapidly." Meade, whom Lincoln had promoted to command the Army of the Potomac just three days before, was 14 miles away in Taneytown, Maryland.

They had arrived the day before on a scouting expedition after Buford learned that the Confederates were in Cashtown. He put together an intelligence report about the enemy's position and activity and sent it by messenger that night to General John Reynolds, who was 11 miles away in Emmitsburg, Maryland. Buford knew it wouldn't take long for Reynolds and his 1st Corps to reach Gettysburg.

Fighting broke out between Heth's and Buford's men

The Union cavalry was on the breaking point when, just before 10 a.m., Reynolds and the 1st Corps arrived. After quickly surveying the situation, Reynolds also sent a note to Meade in which he vowed to "fight them inch by inch, and if driven into the town I will barricade the streets and hold them as long as possible." On hearing this news **MEADE SHOUTED, "GOOD GOD! IF THE ENEMY GET GETTYSBURG, I AM LOST."** Wasting no time, he sent word to the 11th Corps in Emmitsburg, telling it to

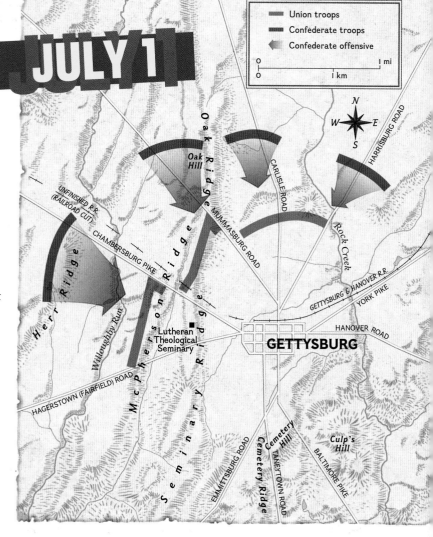

Union troops
Confederate troops
Confederate offensive

0   1 mi
0   1 km

IRON BRIGADE: THE BLACK HATS

The 1st Brigade of the 1st Division of the 1st Corps became one of the Union army's most famous units in September 1862 during the Antietam campaign. Its fierce fighting earned the unit a new name: Iron Brigade. Its men, who came from Wisconsin, Indiana, and Michigan, also were known as the "Black Hat Boys" for the tall, black felt hats they wore. The Iron Brigade took its heaviest losses of the war at Gettysburg, yet continued to fight valiantly. (Of the 1,883 Black Hats who fought on July 1 at Gettysburg, 1,212 were killed or wounded.) The brigade continues to fascinate historians and Civil War buffs because of the valor and tenacity of its men.

move in support of Reynolds's 1st Corps. He also ordered the bulk of the Army of the Potomac to begin marching from Taneytown to Gettysburg. Meade and the rest of the army would follow and set up a new headquarters there, but for now he stayed behind to monitor communications.

Among the first Union troops to reach Gettysburg was the Iron Brigade. Part of Reynolds's 1st Corps, the brigade was made up of regiments from Wisconsin, Indiana, and Michigan. Wearing their distinctive black hats, they marched along the Emmitsburg Road, arriving about 10:30 a.m. Once they got their orders, the men crashed through a woodlot on the western side of McPherson Ridge, pushing the Confederates back. Reynolds stood toward the top of

the ridge, on the eastern edge of the woods, watching the battle unfold below. A Confederate bullet hit Reynolds in the back of the neck. He was dead before he hit the ground. The highest-ranking casualty of the entire battle for both

BATTLEFIELD ART

Many soldiers on both sides drew battlefield maps or scenes of military life in their diaries or letters home. The quality varied with the man. Newspapers and magazines sent professional artists into the field because sketching battle scenes was the only way these events could be visually recorded or published. One such artist was Winslow Homer, who is among the best-known American painters of the late 19th century. Another was Alfred Waud, who made this sketch of the moment General Reynolds was killed. Drawings like this make us eyewitnesses to what soldiers saw and experienced.

sides had been on the field for less than an hour.

Just north of the woodlot, a local shoemaker named John Burns joined the Union line. He was so angry that Confederates were shooting on his town that he went out to McPherson Ridge, picked up a musket from a wounded soldier, and started firing. Never mind that he was 70. He was wounded three times in the fighting that day. (When he died nine years later, the town erected a statue on the battlefield in his honor.) When he thought he might be captured, he crawled away from his gun and told the Rebels that he had been out looking for his invalid wife and got caught in the crossfire.

Meanwhile, the Iron Brigade continued its bloody work against men from Alabama and Tennessee. By 11:30 a.m., Union troops

John Burns

had pushed the Rebels back to Herr Ridge. Private Patrick Maloney of the 2nd Wisconsin Regiment captured Confederate General James J. Archer, to Archer's great humiliation. As Maloney escorted Archer behind the lines, the general encountered an old friend, Union General Abner Doubleday. As was true of many other generals, the two men had served together in the U.S. Army before having to choose sides in the Civil War. "Archer!" Doubleday exclaimed, "I am glad to see you." "Well, I am not glad to see you by a damn sight,"

Archer snapped and refused to shake his friend's hand. Despite seizing Archer, the Iron Brigade experienced its most brutal day of the war on July 1. **ONE REGIMENT LOST 80 PERCENT OF ITS MEN. ALTHOUGH THE BRIGADE ITSELF WAS GREATLY REDUCED, IT CONTINUED TO BE AN EFFECTIVE FIGHTING FORCE.** For the moment, the Iron Brigade and the other Yankee soldiers were able to hold McPherson Ridge.

Over on the north side of the Chambersburg Road and parallel to it, the Rebel troops found a "cut"—a deep trench that had been dug for an as-yet-unfinished railroad. They took cover there and opened a deadly fire on the Yankees who were stumbling back toward McPherson Ridge. Reinforcements soon helped brace the Union line, and Yankees advanced to the edge and eastern mouth of the railroad cut. It was practically a turkey shoot as the Yankees shot down into the cut and along its length. Confederates had little room to maneuver, and the walls of the cut were too steep to climb, but they refused to surrender. Some hand-to-hand fighting broke out, with men swinging their guns like baseball bats. Finally, Lieutenant Colonel Rufus Dawes of the Iron Brigade

A Mississippi color bearer tries to protect his flag from a member of the Iron Brigade near the railroad cut. Carrying the regimental colors was an honor, but a dangerous one.

REGIMENTAL COLORS

Regimental flags, commonly known as "the colors," provided a visual means of communication during the confusion of battle. The flag bearer usually led the troops into battle, giving men a marker to follow and a way for lost soldiers to find their regiment. The color bearer was an easy target for the enemy, though, and capturing the flag was considered a major achievement for the opposing force. The colors often bore the names of the battles the regiment had fought. Like many other Confederate colors, the flag of the 4th Virginia Infantry (below) features the St. Andrew's Cross, which is often mistaken for the national flag of the Confederacy.

collared a Confederate major and demanded that he surrender. To Dawes's surprise, the major did, and Dawes took 232 prisoners. The Rebels who could escape did so by crawling or walking to the western end of the cut half a mile away. The wounded were left with the dead.

Quiet settled over the battlefield while both sides regrouped and waited for reinforcements, which were pouring into the area. During this lull in the action, the Yankees moved to secure the western and northern access routes into town. Their goal was to strengthen their positions by setting up cannon and bringing in as many men as possible as quickly as possible to keep the Rebels at bay.

Yankee hopes were dashed when General Lee arrived on the battlefield about 2:30 p.m. Instead of calling off the fight, he ordered a broad-based attack.

The Confederates started the assault from Oak Hill, northwest of town. Major General Robert Rodes hit the Union line from the side ("on the flank," military people would say) and quickly pushed the Yankees back toward Gettysburg. This was where Samuel Pickens and the rest of the 5th Alabama saw most of their action. Rodes used the regiment to protect the eastern side of his wing. This was not easy going. To get into position, the men had to move through stands of wheat, slog across plowed fields, and climb over fences. By the time they arrived where they were supposed to be, **PICKENS WAS "PERFECTLY EXHAUSTED & NEVER SUFFERED SO FROM HEAT AND FATIGUE IN MY LIFE."** His unit, Company D, was sent ahead to a nearby barn, where they acted as sharpshooters. Once the brigade passed the barn, Company D abandoned the building. Pickens later recalled that, as the men ran to rejoin the brigade, he had never seen "troops so scattered & in such confusion. We were under a heavy fire from the front & a cross fire from the left

& pretty soon had to fall back to a fence where the [brigade] was rallied by Col. [Edward A.] O'Neal and Genl. Rodes." One soldier was killed, four wounded, and five captured.

While Confederate troops pressed toward Gettysburg from the west and northwest, the Union's recently arrived 11th Corps, which included a large number of German-Americans, took up a position just to the west and north of town in an effort to stop Rebels from reaching it. The 11th's chaotic flight from the battlefield at Chancellorsville had earned the corps—fairly or unfairly—the insulting nickname of "the flying Dutchmen." ("Dutch," from the German word *Deutsch*, is what many Americans called Germans at the time.) Unfortunately for the 11th Corps, this would not be a day for redemption. Confederate General Jubal Early's

WAYS TO AVOID SERVICE

The Confederacy started drafting men in spring 1862. The Union followed a year later. These were the first conscriptions (forced military service) in American history. Northerners could avoid the army by paying a $300 fee or by hiring a substitute to take their place. Confederates who held certain jobs—teachers or pharmacists, for instance—and those who owned or worked on plantations with at least 20 slaves also could avoid military service. In both North and South these exemptions led to charges that this was a "rich man's war but a poor man's fight."

SMALL ARMS AT GETTYSBURG

1 **SMOOTHBORE MUSKET** *A muzzleloader with a smooth-walled barrel; fired a round ball (see page 49 top); less accurate than the rifle musket*

muzzle

2 **RIFLE MUSKET** *A muzzleloader with rifling (grooves) in the walls of its barrel; when fired, rifling caused the conical shaped bullet (see page 49 center) to spin, giving it greater range and accuracy than the smoothbore.*

3 **SHARPS RIFLE** *Breechloading gun with a rifled barrel; could be loaded and fired faster than a muzzleloader; fired a paper or linen cartridge (see page 49 bottom)*

breech

4 **REVOLVER** *Carried by cavalrymen and officers; the most popular was the .44 caliber made by Colt.*

27

General Winfield Scott Hancock (pointing) meets with General Abner Doubleday on Cemetery Hill around 3:30 p.m. and orders him to secure Culp's Hill for the Union.

men, which included the 5th Alabama, came down the Harrisburg Road and quickly broke through the line. Although some of the 11th Corps fought courageously, others beat a hasty retreat through the streets of Gettysburg.

Bullets flying through downtown Gettysburg on July 1 left holes in this sign.

Frank Haskell, an aide to a general in the 2nd Corps, was disgusted by reports he heard. "Back in disorganized masses they fled into the town, hotly pursued, and in lanes, in barns, in yards and cellars, throwing away their arms, they sought to hide like rabbits, and were there captured, unresisting, by hundreds." The men of the 11th Corps sought the relative safety of Cemetery Ridge, just south of Gettysburg. "The enemy did not see fit to follow, or to attempt to, further than the town, and so the fight of the 1st of July closed here," Haskell said.

As soldiers from both sides swarmed through the city, residents did not know what to do. "People were running here and there, screaming that the town would be shelled," Sarah Broadhead recalled. Many people hid in their cellars and stayed there for the rest of the battle. Jennie Croll took cover in a bank vault. Bullets and shells zipped through the air, went through walls, and broke windows. Soldiers on both sides called the whizzing noise "music." Civilians were not entertained. "I thought surely we would all be killed in our cellars," Lavinia Bollinger wrote.

Sadie Bushman, the nine-year-old daughter of a cabinetmaker, was supposed to go with her brother to the safety of their grandparents' house a couple of miles out of town. As soon as the two reached the street, they were caught up in the tide of people running away. They traveled about a mile on their own before a Northern officer escorted them the rest of the way. The farm already had been turned into a Union hospital, and immediately Sadie was enlisted to help. She held a cup of water to a soldier's lips as **A SURGEON REMOVED HIS LEG. "I HAD TO SEE THE WHOLE OPERATION, AND I CAN REMEMBER EVERY CUT AS PLAINLY TO-DAY AS I SAW IT THEN,"** she recalled. Because she

was more afraid of the surgeon than the blood, she did not pass out or run away or throw up, but her time as a nurse was "the most fearful" two weeks of her life.

As they chased the Yankees through town, some Rebel soldiers stopped to loot stores and homes. Others fell out of rank to steal money and valuables from dead and wounded Northern troops or demand that local women cook for them. This breakdown in discipline helped keep Lee's army from taking advantage of the rout and finishing off the Army of the Potomac. Nevertheless, the day had been a victory for Lee. It came at great cost, though. He had suffered about 6,500 casualties (men killed, wounded, or taken prisoner), compared with about 9,000 for the North. Arthur Fremantle, a British observer traveling with Lee's army—a common practice in the 1800s—wrote in his diary, "This day's work is called a 'brisk little scurry,' and all anticipate a 'big battle' to-morrow."

A bone saw used by Civil War surgeons to cut through large bones in arms and legs

General William Barksdale urges on his
Mississippians at the Peach Orchard,
where the Rebels smashed through a
Union battalion. Barksdale was mortally
wounded later in the day, near Plum Run.

THE BATTLE: DAY TWO
JULY 2, 1863

"EVERY SQUARE YARD... MUST HAVE ITS BLOOD STAIN."

—LIEUTENANT GEORGE GRENVILLE BENEDICT, 12TH VERMONT REGIMENT

Neither army issued bulletproof vests, but Northern soldiers could buy their own.

When General Meade arrived in Gettysburg in the early morning hours of July 2, he could have made a decision to withdraw and find another place to fight. He did not. Meade liked the lay of the land and thought it gave the advantage to the Union forces, which controlled the hills and ridges east and south of town. To reach them, Confederate troops would have to run uphill and shoot uphill—both challenging. The heights also allowed the Northern soldiers a sweeping view of the area around them. They could see the enemy better than the enemy could see them. Confederate General James Longstreet also recognized the difficulties of storming those hills and the help the terrain gave the Union forces. He begged Lee to move the army elsewhere, pick ground that would work to the advantage of the Confederates, and force the Federals to be the aggressors. The general considered Longstreet's advice and then refused it.

Lee, whose army had arrived in force overnight, noticed that the left, or south end, of the Union line was vulnerable, and he set out to destroy it. His plan was to send 20,000 men under Longstreet's command against the Yankees' southern

BUGLE COMMANDS

The bugle notified men of all kinds of maneuvers, including reveille and drill. "Taps," which Union General Daniel Butterfield adapted for his brigade in July 1862, started as a lights-out call. Other Federal units and even the Confederates quickly adopted the mournful tune, which is now a standard feature of military funerals, wreath layings, and other memorial ceremonies. Every branch of the army—artillery, infantry, and cavalry—used bugle calls during the Civil War, but a standardized system of calls was not developed until 1867.

The bugle is used for communication in the military. The instrument still regulates a soldier's day, but the calls are recorded.

flank and use General Richard Ewell's men to hit Culp's Hill and Cemetery Hill on Meade's northern flank. It was a daring maneuver, but the Army of Northern Virginia had beaten the odds before. The problem now facing Lee was getting his men to their starting points for the assaults, and that took the better part of a hot, humid day.

By the time his men were ready to attack, some were dehydrated and exhausted.

As the Rebels sorted themselves out, the Yankees prepared their defense along Gettysburg's eastern ridges. The bulk of the Army of the Potomac had also arrived overnight. The last corps was still on a 36-mile march to reach Gettysburg that day. Meade set his men in a line the shape of a fishhook, extending from Culp's Hill and Cemetery Hill on the north to Little Round Top on the south. There, on the southern end, General Daniel Sickles, a New York City politician with some military experience but no formal military training, made an unauthorized move. Early in the afternoon he decided to shift part of his line west about half a mile to a patch of high ground where a peach orchard stood. His action stretched his line dangerously thin and—more importantly—left Little Round Top undefended. **THE ROCKY HILL WAS THE MOST VALUABLE PIECE OF LAND ON THE UNION'S LEFT FLANK BECAUSE IT PROVIDED A LOOKOUT FOR MONITORING THE ENEMY.** And unlike Big Round Top, the smaller hill was unwooded on the west side, giving whoever controlled it an excellent place to position their cannon and other artillery. Watching Sickles's line from a nearby rise, Josiah Marshall Favill, a 21-year-old Yankee lieutenant, thought the general's movements were "incomprehensible...very much confused and uncertain." Just as the Confederates started their attack about 4 p.m.,

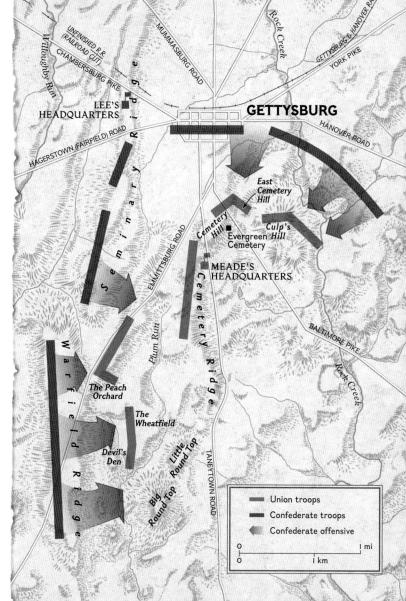

Major General George Sykes—having been alerted to what Sickles had done—hustled a brigade of men from Cemetery Ridge onto Little Round Top to defend it. His quick action came just in the nick of time.

General Longstreet's Rebels slammed Sickles on three sides at once. The fighting and confusion in the Peach Orchard were intense. The din of battle in the area below Little Round Top was deafening, too, and smoke from the cannon and rifles filled the valley that stretched south from Gettysburg. A soldier from a New York regiment on the summit of Little Round Top described the scene as "a great basin…full of smoke and fire, and literally swarming with riderless horses and fighting, fleeing, and pursuing men. The air was saturated with the sulphurous fumes of battle and was ringing with the shouts and groans of the combatants. The wild cries of the charging lines, the rattle of musketry, the booming of artillery and the shrieks of the wounded were the orchestral accompaniments of a scene very like hell itself." Soldiers from each side surged between a wheat field and the Peach Orchard just to the northwest. The Wheatfield alone changed hands at least four times that day.

33

With sword drawn, Colonel Harrison Jeffords of the 4th Michigan lunges to retrieve his regiment's captured flag in the Wheatfield. He got the flag but was fatally bayoneted.

Lieutenant Favill joined the action along the northern side of the Wheatfield, near a small rocky outcrop. **"THE TUMULT BECAME DEAFENING, THE MOUNTAIN SIDE ECHOED BACK THE MUSKETRY, SO THAT NO WORD OF COMMAND COULD BE HEARD, AND LITTLE COULD BE SEEN BUT LONG LINES OF FLAME, AND SMOKE AND STRUGGLING MASSES OF MEN."** His unit, the 57th New York, skirted the fighting "until apparently directly in front of the raging mass of combatants below, then rushed at a double quick boldly forward into the mouth of hell, into the jaws of death," he wrote in his diary. "The fighting was so mixed, rebel and union lines so close together, and in some places intermingled, that a clear idea of what was going on was not readily obtainable." Confusion reigned.

The slaughter was terrible. The battle took a high toll on the officer corps of both armies since those up to the rank of brigadier general were expected to lead their men into battle. Just as Confederate General John Bell Hood's men launched their attack, a shell burst over their commander's head, permanently crippling his arm. Yankee General Samuel K. Zook died after being shot through the bowels in the Wheat-field. Out near the Peach Orchard General Sickles took a cannonball to the leg. As he was carried off the field on a stretcher, he smoked a cigar so his men would not lose heart at the loss of their leader. Neither Sickles's morale-boosting effort nor the reinforcements he received helped. His line broke around 5:30 p.m.

The key to victory on the southern flank lay with Little Round Top. The Yankees had to keep the Rebels from taking it. Confeder-ates raced through a large cluster of boulders below Little Round Top that locals called the Devil's Den. As they headed for the slopes of their prize, Union cannon from the hilltop poured fire onto the rocks. The scene was hellish indeed, yet on the Rebels came. Finally, a group of Yankee infantry, made up of men from Michi-gan, New York, Pennsylvania, and Maine, arrived to stave off the enemy's advance—for the moment.

The arriving Union units were deployed up Little Round Top at a run, and they quickly spread themselves

SICKLES'S LEG ON DISPLAY

After a surgeon amputated his leg, General Daniel Sickles had the limb packed in a box and sent to the Army Medical Museum, where doctors studied battlefield injuries. Attached to it was a card that read, "With the compliments of Major General D.E.S." Sickles remains a controversial figure for his decisions at Gettysburg, but there is no doubt he was colorful. Every year on the anniversary of losing his leg, Sickles would visit the bones. He enjoyed impressing invited guests—especially women. Sickles's bones are still on display at the National Museum of Health and Medicine.

in a thin line along its crest. Just as they got into position, regiments from Alabama and Texas swarmed up the steep, rocky, western slope. These Rebel units, which were thrown into the fray after spending most of the day marching nearly 30 miles to Gettysburg, were exhausted. They had no water with them, which meant they had nothing to quench their thirst and nothing to swish out the gunpowder that got into their mouths when they ripped open cartridges with their teeth—powder that soaked up their saliva, making them even more thirsty. But this didn't keep them from their duty. "When the command was given to charge we moved forward as fast as we could towards the battery" across half to three-quarters of a mile of open field, under fire the whole way, Private John Camden West of the 4th Texas later reported to his son.

The efforts of West and the other Confeder-ates were foiled by the four Union regiments on

Following their color bearer, men of the 5th Texas Regiment scale the western slope of Little Round Top. Fierce fighting nearly won them the high ground.

Little Round Top, including the 20th Maine, commanded by Colonel Joshua Chamberlain. His orders were to "hold that ground at all hazards." Chamberlain sent one company out to guard his left flank from a surprise attack while the rest of his nine companies took cover behind whatever trees or rocks they could find. The fighting was ferocious. The Yankees wavered and their line almost collapsed. They were nearly out of ammunition when Chamberlain ordered his men to fix bayonets. The movement of their charge and pursuit of the Confederates was like that of a swinging gate. Colonel William C. Oates of the 15th Alabama later called the shooting that ensued "the most destructive fire I had ever seen." Caught off guard, **THE REBELS FLED DOWN THE HILL OR SURRENDERED. THEIR ASSAULT ON LITTLE ROUND TOP CRUMPLED AROUND DUSK. THE YANKEES HAD SUCCEEDED IN HOLDING THE FAR END OF THEIR LINE.**

Union troops were under attack elsewhere. Confederate General A.P. Hill's forces nearly broke through the Yankee line on Cemetery Ridge, but the 262 men of the 1st Minnesota plugged the gap, fighting a full Rebel brigade in the process. "Every man realized in an instant [that this] order meant death or wounds to us all; the sacrifice of the regiment to gain a few minutes time and save the position, and probably the battlefield," Lieutenant William Lochren wrote after the war, "and every man saw and accepted the necessity for the sacrifice." Their regiment was the hardest hit of any at Gettysburg, losing more than two-thirds of its men in this fight. That is still the largest single loss of any American military unit that survived a battle. The remaining Minnesotans would fight again the very next day.

Around 6:30 p.m. General Ewell launched his attack on the Union's right flank by advancing on East Cemetery

"FIX BAYONETS"

In a desperate move, Colonel Joshua Chamberlain orders a bayonet charge on Rebels advancing up Little Round Top. Victory went to the Federals.

Two out of three members of the 1st Minnesota were killed or wounded in five minutes as they defended Cemetery Ridge.

about 800 yards to the east. It was late—8 p.m.—when the Confederates charged up the steep, wooded hillside against the entrenched Yankees. After being turned back four times, the Rebels finally gained a foothold on the lower slope. Wesley Culp, who grew up on the hill and for whose family it was named, had moved to Virginia and was fighting for the South. When fighting for the hill resumed the next day, he was killed near his boyhood home.

Darkness did not end the fighting at Culp's Hill, making this one of the few nighttime engagements of the Civil War. Unable to see well despite the full moon, men on both sides had little idea at whom they were shooting. The Confederates hung on through the night and well into the next morning as the Federals pounded away. **"SO TERIFIC [SIC] WAS THE STRIFE THAT SCARCELY A LEAF OR LIMB WAS LEFT ON THE SURROUNDING TREES,"** a Maryland Rebel said. (As a Border State, Maryland officially stayed within the Union, but that did not stop some of its residents from fighting for the South.)

The 5th Alabama had advanced on Culp's Hill, but once

Hill. Ewell was a small, bald, fiery man with a wooden leg, the result of being wounded at Second Bull Run (Second Manassas), in Virginia. He refused to allow the leg to interfere with his ability to lead. When his men were marching, he rode with them in a buggy. When they were in action, he had himself strapped to a horse and commanded from the saddle. On this day he was most definitely in action. Repulsed from Cemetery Hill, he turned his attention to Culp's Hill, a rise darkness fell the regiment was ordered back to town. As far as Pickens was concerned, this was for the best. The regiment had left camp the morning before with 380 men in its ranks. By the end of the second day of battle only 154 were left. The rest were dead, wounded, or missing.

No one who saw or heard the thousands of wounded could ever forget it. Charles Smedley of the 90th Pennsylvania wrote about how one soldier whose legs had been shot off offered a member of Smedley's unit his watch and five dollars to shoot him. Lieutenant George Grenville Benedict of the 12th Vermont Regiment described the nightmarish scenes he observed as he searched for an ammunition wagon that was needed for a morning assault. "I stopped at a dozen or more of the great Pennsylvania barns," Benedict wrote. "Each of them was a field hospital; its floor covered with mutilated soldiers, and surgeons busy at the lantern-lighted operating tables. By the door of one of them was a ghastly pile of amputated arms and legs, and around each of them lay multitudes of wounded men, covering the ground by the acre, wrapped in their blankets and awaiting their turns under the knife. I was stopped hundreds of times by wounded men, sometimes accompanied by a comrade but often wandering alone, to be asked in faint tones the way to the hospital of their division, till the accumulated sense of the bloodshed and suffering of the day became absolutely appalling. It seemed to me as if every square yard of the ground, for many square miles, must have its blood stain."

The end of the second day was a draw, with both sides suffering about 9,000 casualties. Lee had failed to rout the Yankees from key parts of the battlefield: the high ground on the Union's flanks (Little Round Top, Cemetery Hill, and Culp's Hill) and from its center, on Cemetery Ridge.

DEATH BY DISEASE

More than twice as many soldiers died of disease than of wounds during the Civil War. Louis Pasteur's theory that germs caused disease and Joseph Lister's research into the benefits of antiseptic surgery were both still works in progress that would not affect practices in the United States until after the war was over. As a result, Civil War surgeons working in crude field hospitals had no idea that they were spreading disease and speeding infection by not washing their hands or sanitizing their instruments as they moved from patient to patient. One of the few effective medications was quinine, used in treating malaria.

PILULÆ
QUINIÆ
SULPHATIS.
ch containing three grains of
Sulphate of quinia.
PREPARED AT THE
U. S. A.
MEDICAL PURVEYING DEPOT
ASTORIA, L. I.

THE BATTLE: DAY THREE
JULY 3, 1863

"THE ENEMY IS THERE... AND I AM GOING TO STRIKE HIM."

—GENERAL ROBERT E. LEE

Neither army provided soldiers with ID tags, but some men had medallions engraved.

Front

Back

After two days of bloodletting, Lee had a decision to make. His Confederates could make a final stand or they could withdraw, find more advantageous ground, and fight another day. Still confident in the abilities of his men and believing that a victory in Pennsylvania would bring an end to the war, Lee opted to press on. He thought the Union forces were weak around the middle of their line. By sending 12,000 men against the Federals' center, continuing the fight at Culp's Hill, and distracting the Yankees behind their lines with his cavalry—General Stuart had finally arrived in Gettysburg the afternoon before—Lee believed he could smash the Union line and finish off the Army of the Potomac.

The July morning was tense, but—except for the action at Culp's Hill—little shooting took place. By noon the Rebels had failed in their effort to take the hill, and the battlefield went quiet in the sweltering heat. The silence would not last long. A few minutes after 1 p.m., 163 Confederate cannon positioned along Seminary Ridge opened fire on the Union center, which was across the valley on Cemetery Ridge. Corporal George Neese of Virginia said the noise was

Men of the 1st Maryland Regiment burst from the woods at Culp's Hill into a hail of Union gunfire. In the slaughter 56 men and their mascot, a small dog, died.

CANNON AND AMMUNITION

10-POUNDER PARROTT RIFLE
Iron cannon with rifled (grooved) tube; fired canister and the conical shaped ammunition shown below; range: 1 3/4 miles

12-POUNDER NAPOLEON
Bronze, smoothbore (ungrooved tube) cannon; fired canister and round versions of the other kinds of ammunition shown below; range: 1 mile

SOLID SHOT
Solid iron; conical for rifled artillery, round for smoothbore; used at longer ranges against cannon, fortifications, and troops

SHELL
Iron shell (conical or round) packed with gunpowder and fuse; sent out pieces of the metal shell when it exploded

CASE SHOT (SHRAPNEL)
Iron shell (conical or round) packed with metal balls, gunpowder, and a fuse

CANISTER
Tin can filled with iron balls acted like a huge shotgun shell; typical range: 400 yards or less; extreme range: 600 yards

"**A DEEP CONTINUOUS ROLL** OF BOOMING ARTILLERY, SUCH AS AN AMERICAN SOLDIER **NEVER HEARD BEFORE ON THIS CONTINENT.** The artillery fire at one time was so heavy that the hills shook and the air trembled, and the deep thunder rolled through the sky in one incessant roar like as if the giants of war were hurling thunderbolts at each other in the clouds."

Lee had hoped to soften the Union lines with this barrage. It did not work. With every blast the tongues of the cannon carriages dug deeper into the dirt, elevating the barrel of the guns. In addition, some of the ammunition was defective and did not explode on time. Most of the damage to the Union front line was caused by shrapnel and by branches falling from trees hit by solid shot. Sulphury smoke from the guns and dust kicked up by the ammunition filled the area, so Confederate gunners could not see that they were missing their marks. But they were. Their ammunition sailed beyond the front lines by a quarter mile or more, scattering ambulance drivers, hospital staff, and the men who cared for the livestock. The barrage struck General Meade's headquarters, which was on the backside of Cemetery Ridge, several hundred yards behind the line. Errant shells exploded even over the heads of the 5th Alabama's Company D. Once again, Samuel Pickens's unit was acting as sharp-shooters on the edge of town. For a while the Federals fired back with about 80 cannon but then stopped to save ammunition for the infantry charge they knew was coming and to make the Southerners think their guns had been hit.

With his ammunition running out, artillery chief Colonel E. Porter Alexander notified Longstreet that the time had come to begin the infantry assault. Rebel troops gathered among the trees at the edge of open fields a mile or so opposite the Union forces. **ON A SLIGHT RISE THEY COULD SEE A SMALL CLUMP OF TREES—THE HEART OF THE UNION CENTER.** Lee's plan was to break the Union line by having his men drive to its center from several different angles. Between the woods and that copse of trees lay mostly open fields sloping slightly upward toward a rail fence on each side of the Emmitsburg Road and a low stone wall behind which the Union troops waited. It was an excellent defensive position for the Federals.

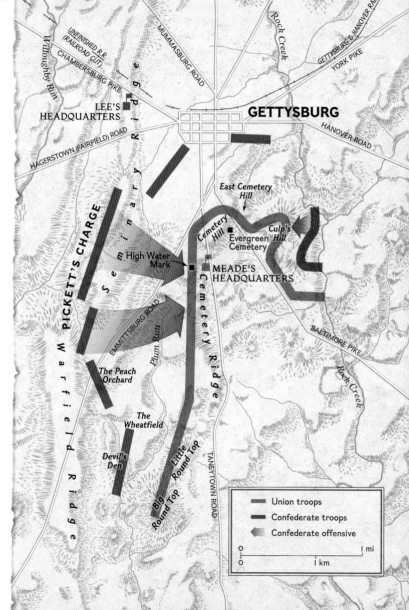

GETTYSBURG

LEE'S HEADQUARTERS

MEADE'S HEADQUARTERS

East Cemetery Hill

Cemetery Hill

Evergreen Cemetery

Culp's Hill

High Water Mark

PICKETT'S CHARGE

Seminary Ridge

Warfield Ridge

Cemetery Ridge

The Peach Orchard

The Wheatfield

Devil's Den

Plum Run

Little Round Top

Big Round Top

CARLISLE ROAD

HARRISBURG ROAD

GETTYSBURG & HANOVER RAILROAD

YORK PIKE

HANOVER ROAD

MUMMASBURG ROAD

Rock Creek

UNFINISHED R.R. (RAILROAD CUT)

CHAMBERSBURG PIKE

Willoughby Run

HAGERSTOWN (FAIRFIELD) ROAD

EMMITTSBURG ROAD

TANEYTOWN ROAD

BALTIMORE PIKE

Rock Creek

	Union troops
	Confederate troops
	Confederate offensive

0   1 mi
0   1 km

Longstreet (with binoculars) and Lee on Seminary Ridge the morning of July 3

The Confederates had nothing but gentle dips in the landscape to protect them from what was sure to be heavy fire. Longstreet hated the plan and had argued strenuously against it when Lee proposed it that morning. According to General George Pickett, Longstreet told Lee to look at "the insurmountable difficulties between our line and that of the Yankees—the steep hills, the tiers of artillery, the fences, the heavy skirmish line—and then we'll have to fight our infantry against their batteries. Look at the ground we'll have to charge over, nearly a mile of that open ground there under the rain of their canister and shrapnel." Lee replied in what Pickett described as "his firm, quiet, determined voice," "The enemy is there, General Longstreet, and I am going to strike him."

LONGSTREET, WHO HAD GREAT DIFFICULTY BRINGING HIMSELF TO GIVE THE MARCHING ORDERS FOR THIS "HOPELESS CHARGE," TOLD PICKETT, "I AM BEING CRUCIFIED AT THE THOUGHT OF THE SACRIFICE OF LIFE WHICH THIS ATTACK WILL MAKE." Pickett, one of Longstreet's division commanders, did not share his superior's worry about attacking the Yankees. Pickett had graduated last in his class at West Point and so far had not distinguished himself in the war. A dandy perhaps best known for his perfumed beard and hair, he was delighted at the opportunity to lead an attack. Besides, he—like so many other Southerners—had complete confidence in Lee.

Rebel divisions under Pickett, Isaac Trimble, and James Johnston Pettigrew stepped out of the woods about 3 p.m. on July 3, with Pickett's Virginians in the lead. Trimble and Pettigrew went with their men, who were from North Carolina, Mississippi, Alabama, and Tennessee. Pickett moved out only part way across the field so that he had a better vantage point from which to direct the charge. The line of soldiers—a mile wide and two or three men

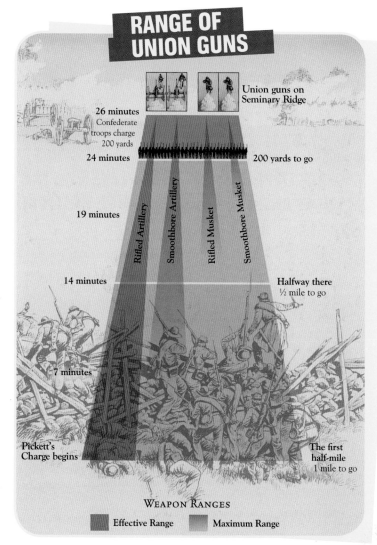

RANGE OF UNION GUNS

Union guns on Seminary Ridge

26 minutes
Confederate troops charge 200 yards

24 minutes — 200 yards to go

Rifled Artillery
Smoothbore Artillery
Rifled Musket
Smoothbore Musket

19 minutes

14 minutes — Halfway there ½ mile to go

7 minutes

Pickett's Charge begins

The first half-mile 1 mile to go

WEAPON RANGES

Effective Range   Maximum Range

deep—marched out of the woods in formation, their guns glistening in the sunlight and their flags snapping in the breeze. "My brave boys were full of hope and confident of victory as I led them forth, forming them in column of attack, and though officers and men alike knew what was before them—knew the odds against them—**THEY EAGERLY OFFERED UP THEIR LIVES ON THE ALTAR OF DUTY, HAVING ABSOLUTE FAITH IN THEIR ULTIMATE SUCCESS,"** Pickett wrote in a letter to his wife the day after. "Over on Cemetery Ridge the Federals beheld a scene never before witnessed on this continent—a scene which has never previously been enacted and can never take place again—an army forming in line of battle in full view, under their very eyes—charging across a space nearly a mile in length over fields of waving grain and anon of stubble and then a smooth expanse—moving with the steadiness of a dress parade."

The Yankee artillery opened fire, sending shells through the Confederate ranks. One shell could kill or injure ten or more men. Artillery also blasted canisters filled with metal balls about the size of quarters, and these, too, took

their toll. As men dropped and gaps opened in the Rebel lines, other men stepped forward to fill the holes. When these soldiers in turn fell, some of Pickett's formations began to wilt.

About 250 yards from the wall, the men of General Pettigrew's division had to scale the split-rail fences along the Emmitsburg Road. As Confederates struggled to clear them, the Federal infantry started shooting. A reliable machine gun was not available during the Civil War, but the effect of firing thousands of Union rifles was about the same. The sight was "terrible," Union cavalry officer Greely S. Curtis wrote a couple of days later, "but we had a strong position and the slaughter of the gray-backs was—what shall I say— awful and splendid. At any rate I saw heaps of dead 30 in a pile...." Mangled bodies, knapsacks, and guns were strewn everywhere. (Some of the guns later found on the battlefield had multiple rounds—bullets, wads, and gunpowder— stuffed down the barrel, meaning that a soldier reloaded in panic, forgetting that he had never fired the previous round. One rifle had 13 bullets jammed in it.) Pettigrew's division buckled. Some Rebels simply surrendered or turned

General Richard Garnett makes a ripe target as he rides toward the Yankee line. He and many of his Virginians were killed before they reached their goal.

GIVE THEM COLD STEEL!

Hat on sword, General Lewis Armistead leads his Virginians over the stone wall that protected the center of the Union line in the final thrust of Pickett's Charge.

back toward the woods where their march had started. Yet, **EVEN AS UNION TROOPS SHATTERED PART OF THE SOUTHERN LINE, MOST OF THE REST OF PICKETT'S MEN KEPT COMING, CLIMBING OVER FENCES, RUNNING ACROSS THE ROAD, AND CHARGING THE STONE WALL NEAR THE STAND OF TREES.**

At the head of a brigade of Virginians was General Lewis Armistead, one of Pickett's subordinates. He led his men with his black felt hat on his drawn sword to make him easier for his men to see and follow. Like many officers who had served in the U.S. Army before the war, he was now confronting men he had attended West Point with and had fought alongside in the Mexican War (1846–48). His good friend General Winfield Scott Hancock was in charge of the very Union troops the Confederate general now faced. When Armistead and his men got within 20 yards of the wall on Cemetery Ridge, some Pennsylvania defenders broke and ran. Two hundred to three hundred Confederates swarmed into the gap and hopped over the wall. General Armistead was still in front of his men, his hat on his sword. It was

DEFINING "HIGH WATER MARK"

The "high water mark" is a controversial designation for the peak of the Confederate efforts at Gettysburg and in the war. The first government historian of the battlefield applied the term to the copse of trees near the stone wall that was a central point in Pickett's Charge. Other people say the mark was where General Armistead was fatally wounded. Still others think it was where a group of North Carolinians penetrated the Union line or where the 11th Mississippi fought. The "high water mark" is probably best understood as a symbol for a nation's hopes rather than an actual place.

about 3:45 p.m. The fighting was fierce, with both sides firing at each other at point-blank range. Armistead was shot two times after he reached the Union cannon beyond the copse of trees. Hancock was shot off his horse as he rode along the front lines, urging on his men. Hancock survived the war, but his wounds were bad enough that he would not return to command until the next spring. Armistead was found and carried off the field by litter bearers. He died two days later.

The spot where Armistead was mortally wounded has come to be known as the "high water mark of the Confederacy" because—although there is some argument about this—it is about as far as the men in gray advanced. Not enough of them penetrated the Yankee line to keep the

SMALL ARMS AMMUNITION

MUSKET CARTRIDGE
This cutaway shows the gunpowder and ball that had to be rammed down the barrel of a musket.

MINIÉ BALL
This lead bullet could be loaded quickly. Its grooves caught those in the rifle barrel, increasing its speed and accuracy when fired.

BREECHLOADING CARTRIDGE
Used in breechloading rifles, this cartridge consisted of a bullet held by a linen or paper wrapper filled with gunpowder.

attack going. As Lee's assault crested and then began to recede, the English observer Fremantle approached General Longstreet behind the lines and said, "I wouldn't have missed this for anything." Longstreet, he recalled, "was seated at the top of a snake fence at the edge of the wood, and looking perfectly calm and imperturbed. He replied, laughing, 'The devil you wouldn't! I would like to have missed it very much; we've attacked and been repulsed: look there!'" After holding out a few minutes, the Rebels began to surrender or fall back in large numbers.

The Yankees continued shooting at those who retreated as long as they were within range. "The fugitives, without distinction of rank, officers and privates side by side, pushed, poured and rushed in a continuous stream, throwing away guns, blankets, and haversacks as they hurried on in confusion toward the rear," recalled Henry Owen of the 18th Virginia Regiment. Trimble and Pettigrew were both wounded. An effort to bring order to the field was overruled by Pickett, who described himself as "weeping bitterly" as he made his way to the rear. "Don't stop any

CUSTER: "BOY GENERAL"

George Armstrong Custer finished last in the West Point class of 1861, but he was very good at self-promotion and politics. For these reasons, along with some military successes, Custer rose to brevet (temporary) brigadier general by June 1863. In a cavalry fight against Jeb Stuart's men just east of Gettysburg on July 3, Custer had two horses shot out from under him and led the charge that ended the Rebel attack. Custer stayed in the army after the war. In 1876 he and more than 200 of his men were killed in a reckless attack on Native Americans camped by Montana's Little Bighorn River.

of my men! Tell them to come to the camp we occupied last night," he ordered.

The great battle was over. Almost 5,600 of Lee's men had been killed, wounded, or taken prisoner in just the last 50 minutes of the fighting. (Over the course of all three days as many as 23,000 Yankees and 28,000 Confederates had been killed, wounded, or captured.) **LEE, WHO BLAMED HIMSELF FOR THE FIASCO OF PICKETT'S CHARGE, RODE OUT TO TELL THE RETURNING SURVIVORS, "ALL THIS HAS BEEN MY FAULT."**

Pickett never got over the loss. Years later he would say, "That old man [Lee] destroyed my division."

The Army of Northern Virginia pulled out of Gettysburg the next day, leaving a few skirmishers behind to protect its rear. Heavy rains from July 4 to July 13 swelled the Potomac River, keeping Lee from

Pelted by a drenching rain, an ambulance train several miles long and full of wounded Rebels meets no resistance from Union forces as it heads out of Gettysburg on July 4.

crossing it. Wounded and trapped, the Army of Northern Virginia was vulnerable to attack while Lee tried to find a way to cross the river near Williamsport, Maryland. But General Meade's caution, logistical problems, and a tired Union force kept the Army of the Potomac from staging anything more than a half-hearted pursuit. Instead, Meade relied mostly on his cavalry to harass the retreating Rebels. Once again one of Lincoln's generals had let slip a chance to finish off Lee.

The Civil War would go on until April 1865, but Lee had suffered such serious losses in Pennsylvania that he would never again be able to go on the offensive, would never again be able to invade the North on a large scale. Gettysburg was not the moment at which the war's outcome became inevitable, but it was a major turning point for both sides.

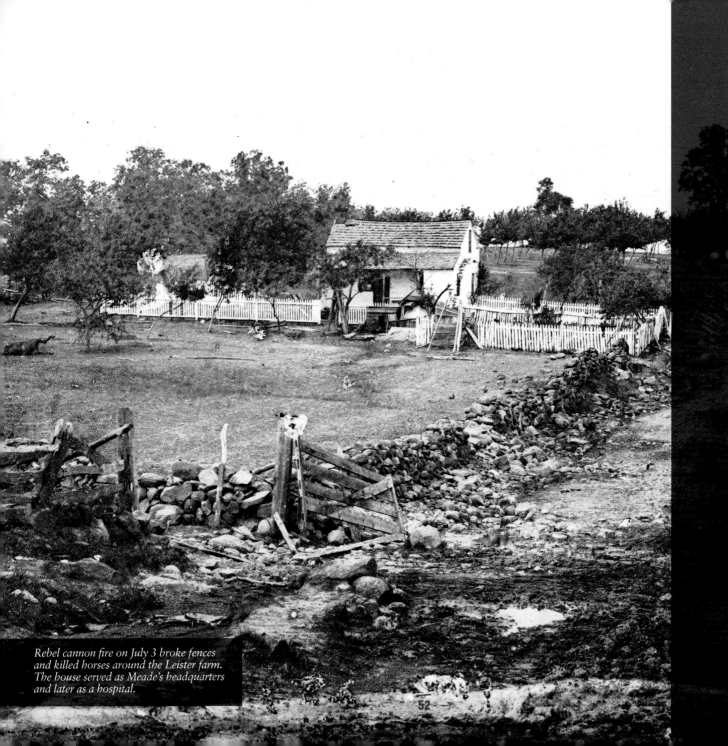

Rebel cannon fire on July 3 broke fences and killed horses around the Leister farm. The house served as Meade's headquarters and later as a hospital.

AFTERMATH

"A PLACE OF PILGRIMAGE FOR THE NATION"

—EMILY SOUDER,
VOLUNTEER NURSE
FROM NEW JERSEY

This spent Minié ball that smashed a clock is among the many collected after the battle.

Rain fell on Gettysburg as residents emerged on July 4, 1863, to survey the damage. Amazingly, with all the bullets and shells that had zipped through the air, only one townsperson had died. Jennie Wade had been baking bread in her sister's kitchen on July 3 when a stray Minié ball pierced the door and killed her. Her family buried her in the garden. Despite the low death toll among the locals, the remains of the battle were overwhelming. Bullets and shells damaged a number of buildings, especially those on nearby farms. Fences were broken, crops overrun, and livestock lost for miles around. Military gear, from canteens to rifles to ambulances, was strewn over the landscape. The town would spend months recovering.

What first struck people after the rain stopped was the smell: the excrement from 165,000 men and from 50,000 to 60,000 horses and mules; the stench of as many as 10,000 dead men and several thousand more animals. The roads were strewn with dead horses. It was midsummer-hot, and the corpses of men and beasts baked in the sun. Black and swollen, they produced odors that would hang over the town for months. One visitor contrasted the "very beautiful, rolling"

Photographer Timothy H. O'Sullivan shot this picture on July 5 or 6. He titled it "Harvest of Death."

Folding embalming tables were easily moved to wherever they were needed.

Pennsylvania Governor Andrew Curtin decided the Union soldiers—not the Confederates—should have a place of honor in which to be buried. The local graveyard, Evergreen Cemetery, was briefly considered as the spot, but a separate area next to it was chosen instead. Attorney David Wills hired landscape architect William Saunders, a Scottish immigrant, to design the soldiers' cemetery. The 18 Union states that had lost men in the battle financed the project. The graves were arranged by state in a semicircle, and no distinction was made between officers and enlisted men. Unknown soldiers occupied each end of the arc.

THE MAN WHO WON THE CONTRACT TO DIG UP, IDENTIFY, AND REBURY NEARLY 3,500 CORPSES RECEIVED $1.59 FOR EACH BODY, WHICH RANGED FROM WELL PRESERVED TO UNIDENTIFIABLE. The crew responsible for this grisly task was made up mostly of African Americans. Whatever Confederate soldiers they found were reburied

countryside to the "awful smell of putrefaction" hovering over Gettysburg. Animals were getting at the bodies. Dealing with the dead became a top priority as concerns of an epidemic rose. Soldiers, prisoners, and townspeople began burying human remains in shallow graves. The bodies of horses and mules were doused in kerosene, then burned—unless they were too close to a building or a tree, in which case they were left to rot. Disinfectant was spread over the streets. It was just another smell to add to the mix.

on the spot; burial crews did not get paid for those men. Families of these soldiers did try to reclaim the bodies, and by the 1870s most had been reburied in the South. No doubt some bodies remain under Gettysburg's fields to this day.

Besides the dead, the town's most pressing problem was the wounded. When the two armies pulled out, they left 21,000 wounded men behind with only about 70 Union medical officers and 35 surgeons and even fewer Confederate doctors to care for them. Hardly a building in town had not been turned into a hospital. Many yards, too, were filled with wounded. Militia Private George R. Frysinger, like many others, wrote, "Gettysburg can not be called a town, but a large collection of hospitals."

Within a couple of weeks the army erected a large general hospital a couple of miles east of town, but Gettysburg's women still nursed a number of wounded in their homes and hosted soldiers' families when they came to check on their loved ones. In both the hospitals and private homes, Confederate and Union men often lay side by side, usually with no friction. Once the railroad was repaired, the wounded who could travel were shipped to army hospitals in Philadelphia, Baltimore, or Washington, D.C., but some

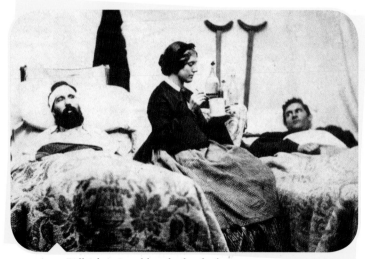
Anne Bell (above) and hundreds of other women on both sides volunteered as nurses during the war.

"ANGEL OF THE BATTLEFIELD"

Clara Barton was a clerk in Washington, D.C., when the war started. She soon realized that the army was not prepared to care for the wounded troops that were being transported to the city and voluntarily began collecting food, clothing, and supplies. As families of soldiers heard about her work, they sent donations. Barton loaded boxes of these goods on wagons and trains headed for battle areas, delivering them herself when possible. Although Gettysburg benefited from her efforts, she never worked there. Called the "Angel of the Battlefield," Barton founded the American Red Cross in 1881.

Edward Everett (holding his hat) was the featured speaker at the dedication of the cemetery for Union soldiers, but it is Lincoln's words that we remember.

CHILDREN OF THE BATTLEFIELD

Amos Humiston of the 154th New York Regiment died in a secluded spot near York and Stratton Streets on the first day of fighting. He was found clutching the ambrotype below, but no one knew his name. The moving story sparked a nationwide effort to identify him, with thousands of copies of this picture circulated throughout the country in newspapers and magazines. Four months later his wife, Phyllinda, identified the picture as being of their three children, Frank, Freddie, and Alice. Public sympathy for the family led to the construction of an orphanage in Gettysburg for the children of slain Union soldiers.

men were wounded so badly they could not be moved. The last would not leave until November.

Northern volunteers mobilized quickly and came to Gettysburg to help with the wounded. They were not the only outsiders to arrive in droves. So did family members desperate to find their fallen soldiers. They would roam the battlefield, looking for their husband's, son's, or father's grave. If they could not find it marked, they would open those that were unmarked. One woman dug up 20 graves before finding her husband's body. Emily Souder, a volunteer nurse from New Jersey, wrote friends that "a perpetual procession of coffins is constantly passing to and fro," and predicted that Gettysburg would become "a place of pilgrimage for the nation."

Already, people were coming as tourists to see where the tremendous battle had been fought and sometimes to look for relics from the fight. The enshrinement of the place started almost immediately. As early as March 1864 charitable groups were asking the people of Gettysburg to donate military material found on the battlefield and to collect even the grass itself; anything from Gettysburg would raise a lot of money, the residents were told. As hundreds of people descended on the town a new question confronted the townspeople: Where would they put them all? Now, besides the wounded, many homes also housed the visitors.

And so it went for Gettysburg until Lincoln pulled into the station on November 18 in his presidential train to speak at the cemetery's dedication ceremony. By the time he left he had sealed Gettysburg's legacy. Never again would the town be an anonymous Pennsylvania community. With the words of his address, Gettysburg transcended history to become a central part of American culture and the American experience. It became not just a place or a battle, but also an idea and an ideal.

TIME LINE

1860

November
Abraham Lincoln, of the antislavery Republican Party, is elected President.

December
South Carolina is the first state to secede (leave the Union). Ten other Southern states eventually follow.

1861

January–February
Seven Southern states form the Confederate States of America (CSA). Jefferson Davis is appointed its president.

March
Lincoln is sworn in as the 16th President of the United States.

April
Confederates open fire on Fort Sumter in Charleston Harbor, South Carolina, launching the Civil War. Remarkably, no one dies during the bombardment.

April–June
Four more states, including Virginia, join the Confederacy. Robert E. Lee resigns his commission in the U.S. Army and joins the Confederate army.

July
Confederates win the first major fight of the war, the First Battle of Bull Run (also known as First Manassas), in Virginia.

August
Rebels win the Battle of Wilson's Creek, Missouri, the war's first major confrontation west of the Mississippi River.

November
The election in the seceded states confirms Jefferson Davis as President of the Confederacy.

1862

February
Union General Ulysses S. Grant gains public attention by capturing Fort Henry and Fort Donelson, in Tennessee.

Jefferson Davis is sworn into office.

March
The ironclad CSS *Virginia* (also known as the *Merrimack*) destroys two U.S. wooden warships and runs three others aground at Hampton Roads, Virginia. A showdown between the USS *Monitor,* another ironclad, and the CSS *Virginia* ends in a draw.

April
The Union win at Shiloh, Tennessee, comes at great cost to both sides. Everyone now realizes the war will be long and bloody.

The CSA Congress enacts the draft.

New Orleans, Louisiana, falls to the Federals.

May–June
In the Shenandoah Valley Campaign the ability of Stonewall Jackson's infantry to move quickly many miles in a day keeps the Union army off balance. Victory goes to the Confederates.

General Robert E. Lee becomes the commander of the Army of Northern Virginia after General Joseph E. Johnston is severely wounded at the Battle of Seven Pines, Virginia (also called Fair Oaks), which ends in a draw.

June
Memphis, Tennessee, falls to the Union.

June–July
In a series of six battles known as the Seven Days Battles, Lee ends the Union's attempt to take Richmond, Virginia, the Confederate capital.

August
The Confederates rout the Yankees at the Second Battle of Bull Run, Virginia. Northern support for the war plunges.

September
The Battle of Antietam (or Sharpsburg), Maryland, ends in a draw. Lincoln claims it as a victory and issues the preliminary Emancipation Proclamation, to be effective January 1, 1863.

December
The Battle of Fredericksburg, Virginia, is another rout for the Confederates. Morale among Union troops, especially in the East, sags.

1863

January
The Emancipation Proclamation goes into effect, freeing all slaves in Confederate-controlled areas.

March
The U.S. Congress enacts the draft.

April
Bread riots break out in Richmond, led mostly by women protesting food shortages and high prices.

Grant begins his Vicksburg Campaign in Mississippi.

May
Lee wins what many consider to be his greatest victory at Chancellorsville, Virginia.

Union forces capture Jackson, Mississippi.

Grant's efforts to take Vicksburg fail; he settles into a siege.

June
North America's largest cavalry fight ever takes place at Brandy Station, Virginia. It ends in a draw, although the Confederates hold the field.

Lincoln appoints General George Gordon Meade to command the Army of the Potomac.

July
In a three-day battle Meade's Army of the Potomac defeats Lee's Army of Northern Virginia at Gettysburg, Pennsylvania. Heavy losses mean Lee will fight the rest of the war on the defensive.

The siege of Vicksburg ends when Confederates surrender on July 4, giving the Union full control of the Mississippi River.

Draft riots break out in New York City. As many as 150 die and more than 2,000 are injured.

September
The Confederates win at Chickamauga, Georgia. Driving Union forces back to Chattanooga, Tennessee, the Rebels begin a siege of the city.

November
Lincoln gives the Gettysburg Address at a dedication ceremony for the Union cemetery at Gettysburg.

General Grant succeeds in breaking the siege of Chattanooga by beating Confederate troops holding Lookout Mountain and Missionary Ridge, high points fringing the city.

The Union victory at the Battle of Knoxville gives the Federals control of most of eastern Tennessee.

1864

March
Lincoln gives Grant command of all Union forces. Grant goes east to travel with the Army of the Potomac. William Tecumseh Sherman takes his place as commander in the west.

May
The Battle of the Wilderness, in Virginia, is inconclusive, but Grant, unlike his predecessors, pursues Lee and fights him in a series of battles stretching into June.

Sherman begins to move toward Atlanta, Georgia.

RESOURCES

June
Lee wins at Cold Harbor, Virginia. A fight at Petersburg, just south of Richmond, leads to Grant's nine-month siege of the city.

The Union Party (formerly the Republican Party) nominates Lincoln for a second term.

July
Confederate General Jubal Early's troops reach Silver Spring, Maryland, just outside Washington, D.C., but are turned back.

The Battle of the Crater at Petersburg, Virginia, ends in a Confederate victory, but the Union siege goes on.

August
The Union victory in Alabama at the Battle of Mobile Bay closes the last Rebel port on the Gulf of Mexico.

Democrats hold their convention in Chicago and nominate George McClellan, former commander of the Army of the Potomac, as their presidential candidate.

September
Atlanta falls to Sherman's army.

Union General Philip Sheridan's scorched earth campaign ensures that the Shenandoah Valley can no longer serve as a food source for the Confederacy.

November
Lincoln is re-elected by a wide margin.

Sherman sets out from Atlanta on his March to the Sea, which will take him across Georgia to Savannah.

December
At the Battle of Nashville the Federals destroy the Army of Tennessee as an effective fighting force.

Sherman takes Savannah and presents the city to Lincoln as a Christmas present.

1865

January
The Union army captures Fort Fisher, North Carolina, giving it access to Wilmington, the last functioning Confederate port on the Atlantic.

The U.S. House of Representatives passes the 13th Amendment, abolishing slavery in all the states. It will be adopted officially on December 6, 1865.

February
Sherman begins his march into South Carolina.

Lincoln and representatives for Confederate President Davis meet for peace talks at Hampton Roads, Virginia, but the discussions go nowhere.

Sherman takes Columbia, the capital of South Carolina. Retreating Confederates start a fire, and Federals add to it, nearly burning the city to the ground.

Confederate troops evacuate Charleston, the city where the war began. The mayor surrenders to Union troops.

March
Lincoln's second Inauguration is held.

Lincoln meets with Grant and Sherman at City Point, Virginia, to discuss how to end the war.

Grant begins his final drive to defeat Lee by cutting his supply lines at Petersburg.

April
Lee withdraws, pursued by Union forces. Jefferson Davis flees as first Petersburg and then Richmond falls.

Lee surrenders to Grant at Appomattox Court House, Virginia, on April 9. The last substantial Confederate fighting forces follow suit at the end of May.

Actor John Wilkes Booth shoots Lincoln at Ford's Theatre on April 14. The President dies the next morning.

ABOUT THE DESIGN

The design of this book, with its use of bright colors, tilted objects, and carefully researched paintings by contemporary artists, is intended as a fresh and lively take on the battle of Gettysburg—one that will grab and hold the reader's attention and make him or her feel more a part of the action. The quote bubbles placed on some paintings were employed as a device to share with the reader words actually spoken by the person at this point during the battle.

RECOMMENDED WEB SITES

On the Gettysburg Address
Library of Congress:
http://www.loc.gov/exhibits/gadd/
Gettysburg Foundation:
http://www.gettysburgfoundation.org

On the battle
National Park Service virtual tour of the battlefield:
http://www.nps.gov/archive/gett/getttour/main-ms.htm
Other National Park Service sites:
http://www.nps.gov/gett/ and
http://www.cr.nps.gov/museum/exhibits/gettex/

On Abraham Lincoln
PBS: http://www.pbs.org/wgbh/amex/lincolns/
Abraham Lincoln Papers:
http://memory.loc.gov/ammem/alhtml/malhome.html
White House biography:
http://www.whitehouse.gov/history/presidents/al16.html
Time line of Lincoln's life, Abraham Lincoln Museum & Library: http://www.alplm.org/timeline/timeline.html

Civil War music, maps, and photographs
American Memory, Library of Congress:
http://memory.loc.gov/ammem/index.html

BIBLIOGRAPHY

Benedict, George Grenville. *Army Life in Virginia : Letters from the Twelfth Vermont Regiment and Personal Experiences of Volunteer Service in the War for the Union, 1862–63*. Burlington, VT: Free Press Association, 1895.

Boritt, Gabor. *The Gettysburg Gospel: The Lincoln Speech that Nobody Knows*. NY: Simon & Schuster, 2006.

Catton, Bruce. *The Army of the Potomac: Glory Road*. Garden City, NY: Doubleday & Co., 1952.

———. *Gettysburg: The Final Fury*. NY: Doubleday, 1974.

Creighton, Margaret S. *The Colors of Courage: Gettysburg's Forgotten History*. NY: Basic Books, 2005.

Favill, Josiah Marshall. *The Diary of a Young Officer Service with the Armies of the United States during the War of the Rebellion*. Chicago, IL: R.R. Donnelley & Sons Co., 1909.

Fremantle, Sir Arthur. *Three Months in the Southern States*. Edinburgh, Scotland: William Blackwood & Son, 1863.

Jones, J. William. *Life and Letters of Robert Edward Lee, Soldier and Man*. Washington, D.C.: Neale Publishing Company, 1906.

McPherson, James M., ed. *The Atlas of the Civil War*. NY: Macmillan, 1994.

———. *Hallowed Ground: A Walk at Gettysburg*. NY: Crown Journeys, 2003.

Neese, George Michael. *Three Years in the Confederate Horse Artillery*. NY: Neale Publishing Co., 1911.

Pickett, George Edward. *The Heart of a Soldier: as Revealed in the Intimate Letters of General George Pickett*. Introduction by La Salle Corbell Pickett. NY: Seth Moyle, 1913.

Sears, Stephen W. *Gettysburg*. Boston, MA: Houghton Miflin, 2003.

Smedley, Charles. *Life in Southern Prisons from the Diary of Corporal Charles Smedley, of Company G, 90th Regiment Penn'a Volunteers, Commencing a Few Days Before the Battle of the Wilderness*. Lancaster (?), PA: Ladies' and Gentlemen's Fulton Aid Society, 1865.

Souder, Emily Bliss Thacher. *Leaves from the Battlefield of Gettysburg: A Series of Letters from a Field Hospital*. Philadelphia, PA: C. Sherman Son & Co., 1864.

White, Ronald C. Jr. *The Eloquent President: A Portrait of Lincoln Through His Words*. NY: Random House, 2005.

Wills, Garry. *Lincoln at Gettysburg: The Words that Remade America*. NY: Simon & Schuster, 1992.

Wilson, Douglas L. *Lincoln's Sword: The Presidency and the Power of Words*. NY: Alfred A. Knopf, 2006.

QUOTE SOURCES

Full bibliographic information is listed only for the first mention of a source not listed in the Bibliography.

Page 12 "a few...remarks" Wills's invitation http://www.loc.gov/exhibits/treasures/images/vc009212.jpg; page 14 "my feet...much" G. Ward Hubbs, ed. *Voices from Company D: Diaries by the Greensboro Guards, Fifth Alabama Infantry Regiment, Army of Northern Virginia*, Athens: University of Georgia Press, 2003, p. 181; "Before the war...anything" ibid., p. 178; page 17 "I was...very much" ibid., p. 181; "some Dutch bread...pretty salt" ibid., p. 179; page 18 "a more unsightly...my heart" Creighton, p. 81; page 21 "a brisk... scurry" Freemantle, p. 129; page 22 "the enemy's force...rapidly" George Gordon Meade, *The Life and Letters of George Gordon Meade, Major-General United States Army*, v. 2, New York, NY: Charles Scribner's Sons, 1913, p. 36; "fight them...as possible" Bruce Catton, *Never Call Retreat*, London: Phoenix Press, 2001, p. 181; "Good God!...lost" Stephen Minot Weld, *War Diary and Letters of Stephen Minot Weld, 1861–1865*, Cambridge, MA: Riverside Press, 1912, p. 230; page 24 "Archer!...damn sight" Sears, p. 172; page 26 "perfectly exhausted...my life" Hubbs, p. 182; pages 26–27 "troops so scattered...Genl. Rodes" ibid.; page 28 "Back in disorganized...hundreds" Creighton, p. 91; "The enemy...closed here" http://www.bartelby.com/43/3501.html, paragraphs 11 and 12; pages 28–29 "People were running...be shelled" Creighton, p. 100; page 29 "I thought...our cellars" ibid., p. 101; "I had to see...most fearful." ibid., pp. 118–119; "This day's work...tomorrow" Fremantle, p. 129; page 31 "every square...blood stain" Benedict, p. 169; page 32 "incomprehensible...uncertain" Favill, p. 245; page 33 "a great basin...hell itself" Allan Nevins, *The War for the Union: The Organized War*, v. 3, NY: Charles Scribner's Sons, 1971, p. 103; page 34 "The tumult...not readily obtainable" Favill, p. 246; page 35 "When the command...battery" John Camden West, *A Texan in Search of a Fight*, Waco, TX: Press of J.S. Hill & Co., 1901, p. 85; "With the compliments...D.E.S." national.healthandmedicine.washingtondc.museum/exhibits/nationswounds/surgery.html; page 36 "hold ...at all hazards" Alice Rains Trulock, *In the Hands of Providence: Joshua L. Chamberlain and the American Civil War*, Chapel Hill: University of North Carolina Press, 1992, p. 133; "The most destructive...ever seen," ibid., p. 144; page 37 "Every man realized...sacrifice" Richard Moe, *The Last Full Measure: The Life and Death of the First Minnesota Volunteers*, St. Paul: Minnesota Historical Society Press, p. 268; page 38 "So terific [sic]...trees" Sears, p. 366; page 39 "I stopped...blood stain" Benedict, p. 169; page 40 "the enemy...strike him" Pickett, p. 94; page 42 "A deep continuous roll... in the clouds." Neese, p. 188; page 44 "the insurmountable difficulties...strike him." Pickett, p. 94; page 45 "hopeless charge...will make" ibid., p. 98; page 46 "My brave boys...dress parade." ibid, pp. 99–100; "terrible...in a pile." Bliss Perry, ed., *Life and Letters of Henry Lee Higginson*, Boston, MA: Atlantic Monthly Press, 1921, p. 203; pages 49–50, 50 "I wouldn't have missed...look there!" Fremantle, p. 272; page 50 "The fugitives...rear" Sears, p. 456; "weeping bitterly...last night." Pickett, p. 99; "All this...fault" Sears, p. 458; "That old man...my division" http://www.encyclopediavirginia.org/Pickett_s_Charge; page 53 "a place...nation" Boritt, p. 16; pages 53–54 "very beautiful...putrefaction" ibid., p. 16; page 55 "Gettysburg...hospitals" ibid., p. 8; page 57 "a perpetual...the nation" ibid., p. 16.

Sources for quotes placed on paintings:
Page 20 words actually spoken by Buford are also the title of the painting; page 30 http://www.brotherswar.com/Gettysburg-2r.htm; page 37 http://www.homeofheroes.com/gravesites/states/pages_af/chamberlain_joshua.html; page 48 words actually spoken by General Armistead are also the title of the painting; page 56 Gettysburg Address.

ILLUSTRATION CREDITS

The National Geographic Society is one of the world's largest nonprofit scientific and educational organizations. Founded in 1888 to "increase and diffuse geographic knowledge," the Society works to inspire people to care about the planet. It reaches more than 325 million people worldwide each month through its official journal, *National Geographic*, and other magazines; National Geographic Channel; television documentaries; music; radio; films; books; DVDs; maps; exhibitions; school publishing programs; interactive media; and merchandise. National Geographic has funded more than 9,000 scientific research, conservation and exploration projects and supports an education program combating geographic illiteracy. For more information, visit nationalgeographic.com

INDEX

Illustrations are indicated by **boldface**.

A

African Americans 12, 17–18, 54
Alexander, E. Porter 43
Ammunition 42, **42**, 49, **49**, 53, **53**
Amputation 29, **29**, 35, **35**, 39
Archer, James J. 24–25
Armies, parts of **22**
Armistead, Lewis **6**, 48, 48–49
Art, battlefield 24, **24**

B

Barksdale, William 30, **30**
Barton, Clara 55, **55**
Bell, Anne 55, **55**
Benedict, George Grenville 39
Bollinger, Lavinia 29
Brady, Mathew 13
Broadhead, Sarah 29
Buehler, Fannie 18
Buford, John 20, **20**, 21–22
Bugles 32, **32**
Bulletproof vests 31, **31**
Burns, John 24, **24**
Bushman, Sadie 29
Butterfield, Daniel 32

C

Cannon 42, **42**, 45, **45**
Casualties 8, 29, 50, 53–55, **54**, 57
Cemetery Hill 28, **28**, 32, 38, 39
Cemetery Ridge **4–5**, **6**, 28, 36–40, **38**, 42–46, 48–50
Chamberlain, Joshua **6**, 36, 37, **37**
Chancellorsville, Battle of 15, 16, 27
Confederate Army
    avoiding service 27
    casualties 29, 54–55
    hardships 14, 16–17, 18, 35
    retreat from Gettysburg 50–51, **51**
    shoes 14, **14**, 17, 18
    uniform and gear 17, **17**
Confederate currency 18, **18**

Croll, Jennie 29
Culp, Wesley 38
Culp's Hill 28, 32, 38–39, 40, 41, **41**
Currency 18, **18**
Curtin, Andrew 54
Curtis, Greely S. 46
Custer, George Armstrong 50, **50**

D

Dawes, Rufus 25–26
Devil's Den 35
Dilger, Hubert 7
Disease 39
Doubleday, Abner 24–25, 28, **28**
Draft 27, **27**

E

Early, Jubal 18, 27–28
Everett, Edward 56
Ewell, Richard 32, 37–38

F

Favill, Josiah Marshall 32, 34
Flags 8, **8**, 9, **9**, 25, **25**, 26, **26**, 34, **34**, **36**
Fremantle, Arthur 29, 49–50
Frysinger, George R. 55

G

Garnett, Richard 47, **47**
Gettysburg, Pa. **6**, 18, 28, 28–29, **52**, 53–54
Gettysburg Address **6**, 9, 10–13, **56**, 57
Gettysburg Cemetery 11, **11**, 13, **13**, 54
Guns **16**, **17**, 27, **27**, 45, **45**
    See also Cannon

H

Hancock, Winfield Scott 28, **28**, 48, 49
Haskell, Frank 28
Heth, Henry 21, 22
Hill, A. P. 36–37

Homer, Winslow 24
Hood, John Bell 34
Hospitals 29, 39, **52**, 55, **55**
Humiston, Amos 57

I

Identification medallions 40, **40**
Iron Brigade 23, 24–26, **25**

J

Jeffords, Harrison 34, **34**

L

Lee, Robert E. 8, **15**, **44**
    confidence in 45
    confidence of 15, 16, 40
    scouting reports 18–19
    strategy 26, 31–32, 40, 42, 43–44, 50
Lincoln, Abraham 9, **10**, 10–13, **13**, **56**, 57
Little Round Top **6**, 32–33, 35–36, **36**, 37, **37**, 39
Lochren, William 37
Longstreet, James 31–32, 33, 43, **44**, 44–45, 49–50

M

Maloney, Patrick 24
Maps **6**, 12, 19, 23, 33, 43
McPherson Ridge 20, **20**, 21–25
Meade, George G. 9, **22**, 22–23, 31, 32, 42–43, 51, 52
Money 18, **18**

N

Neese, George 40, 42
Nurses 55, **55**

O

Oak Hill 7, 26
Oates, William C. 36
O'Neal, Edward A. 27
O'Sullivan, Timothy H. 54
Owen, Henry 50

P

Peach Orchard 30, **30**, 32, 33, 35
Pettigrew, James Johnston 45, 46, 50
Photography 13
Pickens, Samuel 14, 17, 26–27, 39, 43
Pickett, George 44–46, 48, 50
Pickett's Charge **6**, 45, **45**, 46, 47, 48, **48**, 49

R

Reynolds, John 20, **20**, 22–24, **24**
Rodes, Robert 26, 27

S

Saunders, William 54
Seminary Ridge 40, 42–43, 44, **44**
Shenandoah Valley, Va., map of 19
Sickles, Daniel 32–33, 35, **35**
Slavery 12, 14, 17–18, 27
Smedley, Charles 39
Souder, Emily 57
Stuart, "Jeb" 19, **19**, 40, 50
Sykes, George 33

T

Trimble, Isaac 45, 50

U

Union Army
    avoiding service 27
    range of guns 45, **45**
    reasons for fighting 12–13
    uniform and gear 16, **16**, 31, **31**

W

Wade, Jennie 53
Waud, Alfred 24
West, John Camden 35
Wheatfield 33, **34**, 34–35
Wills, David 11–12, 54

Z

Zook, Samuel K. 34–35